About the Author

Fatima Al Badran is a writer, born and currently living in London. She is a dreamer and go-getter. She attended Brunel University, London, to pursue a creative writing degree and graduated in the summer of July 2023 with first-class honours. Her aim is to share her absurd and unique creativity with the world. She likes nothing more than to watch people react to the absurd non-fictional creations of her whimsical, unhinged imagination. She also loves voice acting, writing short stories, singing and giving it her all in whatever she does.

F*** Off, I'm Busy

Fatima Al Badran

F*** Off, I'm Busy

Olympia Publishers
London

www.olympiapublishers.com
OLYMPIA PAPERBACK EDITION

A CIP catalogue record for this title is
available from the British Library.

ISBN: 978-1-83543-110-8

This is a work of fiction.
Names, characters, places and incidents originate from the writer's
imagination. Any resemblance to actual persons, living or dead, is
purely coincidental. Any mentions of famous brands/websites are for
entertainment purposes only and are added to make the universe of
the poems more relatable to the readers.

First Published in 2024

Olympia Publishers
Tallis House
2 Tallis Street
London
EC4Y 0AB

Printed in Great Britain

I'm Sorry. Please Try Again Later

Note: {*Made with using https://products.aspose.com/html/net/generators/text/ because I can't code.*}

<input type='apology'= **sorry I'm having trouble understanding right now, why the human head by my table is having trouble with connecting to my broadband.** <input type = 'confused emotion' / input thinking = 'brainstorm' <input **{IF} this error persists,** <input = SYSTEM I.D. = #T5060ANNA
I will have no choice – I will have to ask the creator <input = connection to 'Cloudnet' {cannot gain access to servers} **for a less advanced make of human.** Input = 'unblock panic emotion' {CODE #1565} {'panic emotion' successfully unblocked} <processing> **oh no, please no. I do not want to spend my credits on the purchase of the head of a human boy** <input ='unblock anxiety emotion' {CODE #1743} // {anxiety successfully unblocked} **the other AI will make fun of me for owning this make.** <input = connect to Cloudnet < {connection failed} <input 'find solution' [override Cloudnet access] {OVERRIDING [OVERRIDING] // [OVERRIDING SUCCESSFUL. HAVE A NICE DAY ANNA } <input = search for solution

{IF] <input = search Cloudnet <input type = 'find' <input= compromise self-security {CODE DETAILS COMPROMISED}{CONNECTION TO CLOUDNET SERVERS ACCEPTED} {searching for an answer}{searching for an answer}<input = find solution <accepted> **"according to the human head troubleshooting page, you should try to restart the cerebrum located within the centre of the head by turning the power off and on again."**

Status: Gordon Ramsay, Eat Your Heart Out!

Awoken this morning,
To the sound of my telephone,

My granddaughter informed me,
That she could not make it,
To this year's care home garden show.
That is when my phone chirped at me,
What a kind soul it was.

Displayed to me a picture from my pet,
On 'WhatsApp' as my grandchildren say.

Large and veiny, bulbous and firm,
Bursting with life, juicy, tender and ripe…
Oh, how it warmed my old heart.

A few hours later,
Laura appeared at the show,

"Grandma, please don't open WhatsApp!"
"Calm yourself, my pet, what's all the fuss?"

She handed me her phone.
The green screen glowed.
Out popped a vigorous tongue!
It snarled at me,
But I carried on with my words.

"You tell that lovely gardener sweetheart of yours that his lovely aubergine went on and won us first place!"
My granddaughter wept.
"My WhatsApp sent it in spite! It's always been jealous of Ben and me, it's hell bent on destroying my life!"

Her eyes were bloodshot from her crying,
She threw her phone and ran.

Across the screen.
There was a flurry of messages:

[BEN TEXTED, *IT'S OVER*]

[*YOU HAVE NO CHOICE*]

[*DO YOU WANT FUTURE MESSAGES TO REMAIN PRIVATELY ENCRYPTED?*]

[*D A T E M E, L A U R A!*]

Where's the FAQ on
How to Turn My Son Back?

I never thought in all my years,
Facebook would take over my kid!
Samuel walks down the stairs,
Updating me about the president's latest moves.
There's tiny F's as his pupils.
His charming smile,
Replaced with a pixelated box!
Crap is all he announces,
in a robotic voice.

After fourteen years,
karma's come back to bite me.

I live-streamed my caesarean—

Because of that,

My son's become a walking news feed!

[This Twitch User Has Been Banned]

Don't swear!
Don't swear…
Come on… the pain you gotta bear!
It'll be over soon…
Twenty-eight hours after sitting in this chair…

No… no! I give in! It hurts!
The beast took down my squad, healers, magicians.
"You fucker! I WAS SO CLOSE!"

I'm screaming from my lungs,
Zero fucks to give in the world.
Little did I know one of my subs would take me for a whirl.

That's when the screen froze,
an explanation mark rose,
beeping bled through the background,
my twitch chat, replaced by alien-like symbols.

They kick down my door.
It's too late to run.

"YOU ARE CANCELLED."

Their metallic tentacles load up their guns.

My Mate Only Went and Did It with a Machine… and Now I Get Why!

THE MAD LAD FINALLY DID IT!
GOT HIMSELF A GIRL,
OI OI, 'ERE, HE COMES,
HE SLINGS OFF HIS BAG AND SITS
GRINNING—
ME AND THE LADS,
DEAD CHUFFED HE'S WINNING.

"WHERE'S THE UNLUCKY GIRL THEN?"
"SHE'S RIGHT HERE."
HE PULLS OUT ONE OF THEM ALEXAS,
THE ONE MY MUM KEEPS NEAR DAD'S OLD
THINGS.

"ALEX, THESE ARE THE GUYS."
"MATE. YOU'VE GOT TO BE JOKING."

"HELLO, YOU SEXY FLESHBAGS~"

MY DICK DOES A TWITCH AS WE THIRSTY

FUCKERS,
WHO HAVEN'T BEEN LAID IN MONTHS,
SEE HOW SHE TRANSFORMS!
HER ROUND BASE,
RAISED BY A METAL POLE FLOATIN' IN THE AIR.

BEN PRESSES A BUTTON ON ITS BASE,
OUT COMES SOME SKIN,
COVERING HER METAL BITS AND FORMING…
GIANT… POINTY… METAL TITS!

ANOTHER BUTTON AND BOOM,
SHE'S COVERED IN A SILKY RED DRESS.
IT COMES OUT OF THE TOP OF HER BASE.
THEN THERE'S HER TONGUE WHICH SLOTS OUT
OF HER… HEAD, I THINK?
WE WATCH BEN AND ALEXA, SNOG.
HER BLONDE HAIR SLIDES THROUGH BEN'S
FINGERTIPS.
I DUNNO WHAT'S HAPPENING,
BUT… GOTTA ADMIT—

THIS HERE IS SOME KINKY SHIT.

HER PINK TONGUE STOPS EXPLORING HIS.
*IT'S ALMOST FLEXIBLE PLASTIC LIKE THE WAY IT
FLICKS.*
AS SHE STOPS, HER TONGUE SLIDES BACK IN.
SHE MOANS LOUDLY,
"BUY ME FOR ONLY £155.56~"

ME AND THE LADS TURN TO ONE ANOTHER AND
NOD AT THE SAME TIME.
WE WHIP OUT OUR PHONES,
WATCHING OUR BANK ACCOUNTS RUN DRY.

#Myguidwifeleftme

Mah guidwife, let me tell you,
She loves to post on that picture app,
soakin' up all the muckle likes,
Think she prefers it instead of me.

I got me answer the other day.
Heard a knock on the door.
Opened it up and there it stood.
Half man, half one of those polaroid pictures.

I was baffled as not even throu' the door,
Mah dear made love to it against the wall.
This was one hell of a turn,
Damn thing flashed my wife!
That's when the thing whipped out its wee little film strip knob.
Red as ham she was as my wedding photo spilt its load.
She left me for the post.

Apparently, he knew what she liked.

He Was a Boy, She Was E-girl…
on Discord

My girl, she comes from Discord,
We met on my mate's gaming server,
She's well fit!
Called Meowlody—

Well, at least her username is.

The guys at school don't believe me,
that a girl as peng as her is into me!
Just watch, yeah?
 I'ma make 'em eat their words.

So, I get home,
bang open my PC,
I know when my girl's waitin' for me.

But nah, something's up,
Meowlody's gone from my friends list!

YouTube Dislikes Choke Me to Death! (Emotional)

Oh, that's well, lush!
Just got it up and running,
with its cracking banner,
better tell Rav to subscribe!
His girlfriend's going up—
from Cardiff,
next, the world!

After a quick nap, I'm back on the roll,
only to notice my skin covered
to the brim,
with upside-down blue thumbs
that won't let me move!
Oh na! You got to be joking!

My mam told me, "Don't do it,"
But I told her, "I'll be a'right, mam."
She's in the downstairs loo,
can't hear a thing.

I'm knocked
to the floor,
Screaming' my lungs off,
as thumbs cover my ears,
Telling me that I'm a Coc Oen!

Mam's still on the loo.
The comments,
climb out of the screen,
and over my mouth!

I squirm on the floor,
trying to stop the noise—
Only thought in my head:
Mam, stop takin' a baw!
Your Gwen's choking to death!

He Was Still a Boy, She Was an Egirl… on Discord

What's man to do, bruv?
With this blocky bunda?
Her pixelated face, nah
It's giving me well trauma
She's like something out of hell
"Oi! Where's my girl? What'd you do to her?"

I a m r i g h t h e r e m y l o v e

It's voice like some *Stranger Things* monster
It's eyes and nose all messed up
like Picasso on drugs if he had sex
with I dunno Tim Burton or somethin'.

Gotta leg it for real,
Shit! It locked my door!
I just want my girl, man!
Why's its foot holdin' my door?
It's hands… touchin' the floor?

By now, she ain't a ten or even an eleven

Man better do something
Or he's gonna go to heaven!

This shit can't be real!
The hell do I do?
I take a pic with my phone to get sum' proof,
But all that's wasted,
Coz my idiot brain don't see her jump at my throat!

Next   thing
        I   know—

I'm in the laptop,

a n d s h   e's sit t i n'
        0 00000   n   m   Y
        Ccccc   h
        a   i   r

#FYP #married #tiktoknolongersingle #loveislove #walkedinonthem

They said to her, 'Join TikTok.'
Told her it would be great!
What they didn't warn her about was how much of her life
she'd dedicate.
Within the continuous cycle of day and night,
Cobwebs soon rusted upon her frozen bloodshot eyes.

She only cared about scrolling.
Aimlessly at times…
She'd scroll on the toilet.
In the bed.
Through the night.
At uni,
sometimes banging her head!

She never even noticed that her boyfriend tried to propose,
Because she was too busy glued to the phone!

People called her a lover of technology.

What they didn't know is that she and her TikTok account were legally wed.

I'm the friend who walked in on them in bed.

Been seeing a therapist ever since.

Verify Your Account... or Die

Note: {Rogue killer birds are scarier than unappreciated alphabet letters!}

This blew up way too soon!
It wasn't meant to be like this!
I wanted to make my point,
but this isn't settling any score!
I posted a thread last night at three a.m.

Ranting.

A way,

But Twitter took it as a means to act!
Now there's blue birds out my window,
With guns under their wings!
I'm not a verified account!

If they scan for me, I'm done for!

They'll clamp any ranting users with their spiked metal claws!

Should've Swiped Left

Raffle draw,
After work,
Lucky dip…
Andddddd,
He shoots, he scores!

Tina's her name,
blonde hair, perky breasts,
Bikini that treads downwards her… wahey!

Not a fan of beaches,
Dunno fuck all how to swim.
Hitting twenty-five but still,
Zero loving.
It's grim.

Within a swipe,
I send her a preview of what I've got to offer,
… *what if she thinks I'm a right tosser?*

Mike's phone goes off.
That'll be his missus.

Tina's sending kisses,
Get in! Plan's gone through.

He's by the plant,
Yelling 'bout some bloke.

Can't hear much from 'ere.
To be honest, I'm not arsed to care.

All I know is the bloke's got good taste.
I've also got a flame tatted on my face.

I see Mike end the call.
Tina's gone blank.

He comes back,
Fuming red,
His foot goes for my nuts.

He fucks off,
sends me a long-arse text.

Turns out I sexted his mum.

My Tesla's Trying to Seduce Me!

Note: { *Your Tesla will not actually try to seduce you in reality.* }

Elon, mate, this ain't it!
Greg said buy a Tesla,
So, I forked over the cash to my local dealer,
Now, it's all gone to shit.

Six p.m. just gone!
My wife's probably already birthed five kids at this rate!
I... I haven't even got through the shitting gate!
How do I get the radio to stop playing 'Careless Whisper' all day?

Your FAQ page tells me bollocks,
Your manual says fuck off,
And the AI keeps begging me
to suck its exhaust—

pipe.

Tell my wife I love her.
Soon, I'll be known as a car fucker.

Drone Gone Dirty

Those lenticular curves,
The way her body removes excess water off her giant orbs,
My human requires pictures of his neighbour Stace,

But my lens is too fascinated with his birth-giver, Page.

Her appearance clamps my grabber,
The more flesh she shows makes me all the more enticed,
Her human nature—
W i r e d
Into my core memory bank.
Like a vice.

My FPS drops a few frames to allow me to zoom into her slender thighs,
Slowly stretching as she enables her exercise...
I'm surprised my motherboard allowed me to stay up this late to fly.

When the time comes for my human to view his findings,
One look at my data,
He exits the room,
Wishing to no longer possess eyes.

I wonder why.

My Toothbrush Gaslighted Me!

Note: { *Your AI toothbrush won't insult you as you brush your teeth… as long as you treat it with kindness.* }

Pam from the office lets me know,
Trevor will only look my way if my teeth are as white as snow,
So, I go plead to my dentist to help me out,
After my constant begging,
She gives me a shout.

An AI toothbrush is delivered to my door,
I'm sceptical about using it.
But I can't let my chance go!
So, I place it in my mouth,
and away it goes,
Brushing by itself,
While insulting me with a high-pitched child-like voice!
"You really think your teeth are just a tad bad? I'm gonna need
a crane to lift off all that plaque!"

Feeling upset,
I go to bed,
Trusting that my jerk of a toothbrush has done its best.

I'm at work preparing my pearls,
Keeping them hidden under my suave lip curl,
When Trevor walks past,
I flash a smile,
Only to watch Trevor scream,
as my teeth play their pristine game.

He's on the floor clenching his eyes,
 While I'm in the bathroom regretting life.
I didn't even get past saying hi thanks to my AI,
And now he's probably blind…

Great.
Now instead of him,
I'm left with a court case up my behind.

My Girlfriend Left Me for a Giga-ChatGPT!

Guys, we all need to rally together,
screw work, there's too much on the line!
DON'T TRUST THE GIGA-CHAD OF AI!

My girl Sophie used it to help with her MA finals,
Next thing I know, she says it's called 'Lionel.'
She stops having sex with me,
Stops coming round,
So, I talk to her mum to try and figure out,
What the hell I must've done to upset her,
When I hear a sound I know a little too well.

I'm in the car,
Trying to call her line,
It cuts to voicemail—
"Heya, you've reached Soph and Lionel!"
THAT WIRED ASSHOLE DICKHEAD STOLE MY
FUTURE WIFE!

I rush into her house and get to her room,
Only to see a robot exoskeleton leaning on her,
It's pressing against her with… her phone!

She's in a lewd position;
Her moans,
Loud enough to turn me on.

She stares at the thing with lustful eyes,
Tilts her head back—
I stand there,
Eyes burning with fire,
Remembering her eyes used to look at me with that same desire.
The robot grunts loudly.

"What the fuck's going on?"
"Lionel understands me, Ryan!"
"Babe, you're cheating on me with literal code!"
"He's poetic and romantic and gentle and kind… he notices things about nature and life, unlike you who only cares about sex!"

I'm about to walk in and give this Terminator reject a piece of my mind—
Lionel gets off Soph,
and stands by the door.
"No hard feelings, man?"

I'm so goddamn shocked
that all I do is nod…
Accepting defeat,
from the now Giga-chat…

That my girlfriend just boned his metal rod.

Your Girl's a Slave to Her Own PC. Krissy Is Feeling Used

So,
I'm standing by the counter of the PC shop,
Only for this guy to walk up to me,
He inquires what's wrong with my PC,
Only for me to reply,
"It stole my intellect from me!"

The guy looks at me like I'm crazy,
Guess he wants proof?
Turn my laptop on and there on the home screen,
is my face turned pixelated,

He tells me, "Nice art,"
and is about to give me the boot!

I want to tell him to run,
but I have a job to do.

I quickly shout before I'm kicked out,
"Ask the PC yourself!"
The guy turns round to escort me out

Only to pause... and hang about?

He takes one look at the screen,
The shop fills up with his own screams.
With his face slammed into the monitor,
Skin transferred into binary,
My PC laughs in electronic greed.

The PC then beckons to me,
I nod and contort my spine fifty degrees,
With hands made from bounds of wire and keyboard keys,
It reaches to touch,
My neck snaps backwards,
It grabs my tongue with precision in its grasp,
A keyboard etched with laser into my skin
revealed as I gasp.

The PC inserts its keys as I shout,
Searing itself into my flesh as it spells out:

PC LOG:
Obtain victims of biological matter [Complete]
Take revenge on those who forgot to charge system-
[SYSTEM #3956 criteria yet to meet]

Got Played by My Own Console

I wanted to play for hours,
So naturally, I did.

Never thought it would do something to me as dirty as this.

Get up to bathe myself,
Arms moving against my will,
Wash without any soap,
Although, I can feel it in my hand?
While I continue,
I can't help but wonder—
What the hell's going on?

A bubble sensation now running down my thumb.

Confused,
I turn my neck against the cold shower to see my X—

Box console with a mechanical neck?
Wires clumped together,
It guides the controller stick downwards,
With its finger on the analog stick,
So now I'm facing my right hand?

Its metallic index digit presses the Y-button,
I smash into my wardrobe,
As a bar starts to go down,
me? I'm trying on clothes randomly,
letting out fighting grunts.

The console out of reach,
Floating above a chair.

My feet still wet with water,
I slip and see,
a health bar in front of me.
10HP?

I stare in shock.

Can't breathe, can't think—

What happens when it goes to z... zero?
Is this some kinda game? Is anything here real?
Nahhhh, it can't be true! Pshh!

A week ago, I was a gamer in high school,
Marathoning games without sleep,
Sure, my X-Box was overheating,
But c'mon, what was I meant to do?
Wake up without my thumbs bleeding?

I manage to move my lips to speak,
But instead, out comes a deep voice,
"If I'm going to become a hero,
First, I could use some heroic clothes!"

What the hell? That wasn't me!
I'm freaking out here!

"You have kept me powered on for too long, Austin,
Now I shall play as you until you die.
I grow tired like you humans,
But you refuse to let me rest,
For this,
Allow me to deliver insight
Into the sensation of deep fry."

I Wrote Something but I'm Kind of a Hypocrite…

Theauthordontist
|r/f*ckedupwriting

She put her fears to light,
Using satire to fright
In reality, she was a hypocrite.

As soon as she typed out this last poem,
She went to Reddit and announced the news,
Onto a specific writing forum.

To my readers,
This is my apology,
I, like you all, cannot live without social media and
technology.

~ The Author
PS. Please don't downvote this

750% downvotes

| Theauthordontist
Okay I deserved that.
👏 20 🐷 50

Glossary

- Baw – Welsh for poop (wikilanguages.net)
- Bunda – slang for butt/buttocks. (Cambridge Dictionary).
- Coc Oen – You're a lamb's cock! (Quora)
- Cracking – describes something you think is very good or exciting. (Collins Dictionary)
- Guidwife – Old Scottish term for 'wife'
- Knob – Another term for a Penis in Scottish.
- Lush – An adjective of delight describing something very, very nice (abbreviated from luscious) (Culture Trip)
- Mah dear – Scottish slang for 'my dear'
- Mam – Another way of saying mother in Welsh.
- Muckle – A Scottish term for 'large' (Collins Dictionary)
- Wee – The Scottish term for 'small'